Rebecca Bloom

MPS, LMHC, ATR-BC

This book is dedicated to
Dr. Christine Blasey Ford,
your testimony broke me open,
and the paintings in this book flowed out.

Vicarious Trauma
  the taking on of
  the symptoms of our clients.
You cannot sleep,
  You do not want to go to work.
you have no energy
    to do fun things.

You're irritable.
you have nightmares.
You're afraid to go places.

Burnout, compassion fatigue, vicarious trauma, in this book I will lump them all together as the experience of Vicarious Traumatization. It is most often explained as, when you do the work of helping others, beginning to experience their symptoms—hopelessness, fear, insomnia, and so on.

The term vicarious trauma was first coined in the nursing profession. It was found that,

> "Expectation that providing a specific level of care will ultimately lead to positive outcomes for every patient is not only unrealistic and naïve, but may set nurses up for stress when they are unable to meet their expected goals"
> (Laschinger & Finegan, 2005; Leiter, 2005).

This expectation, that every interaction will go perfectly and lead to a positive outcome, can be found across many fields these days. Anyone who works with people knows that this is an impossible standard to meet, and when addressing the complicated experience that is human behavior change, things often progress in a non-linear fashion. It is a long process with setbacks and literal falls off the wagon. By dropping the expectations and allowing for more room for what actually happens in the work, professionals can feel they have room to grow, moving from a traumatic stress model to a traumatic growth model. The work of being a counselor is hard, sometimes unrewarding, and even scary work. It asks that we as practitioners continue to not just gain the skills to do the work, but also look deeply, sometimes painfully at who we are now, the world around us, the families we grew up in and family patterns, sometimes going back multiple generations.

When the field becomes so focused on measurable outcomes and documentation, practitioners have no time to talk about how the work is impacting them. All students and early professionals are supposed to get an hour a week of Supervision with an experienced Clinician. That time is meant to be spent talking about the young professionals experience with clients. These days, if it happens at all, that time is about making sure your paperwork is done correctly so that organizations continue to get funding. I believe this is one of the major reasons why across the field of mental health, 50% of folks with a master's degree are not in the field after two years and another 25% are done after five years. (I wish I could remember where I got this statistic from, but anecdotally, is seems true).

I taught in a Masters in Art Therapy program for eight years. In my first year teaching, I noticed that some of the students I enjoyed the most never practiced in the field after graduating. They were so burnt out by what they had experienced at their two-day-a-week internship, working as a therapist and interacting with the state-funded mental health system, that they did not want to do the work they had just spent two years studying. This made me incredibly sad. I hoped to combat this by putting more focus on Vicarious Trauma during lectures and readings during class time. In a search for protocols to address this experience, I came across Karen Saakvitne's work and a nine-question questionnaire she had developed that looked at the experience of the clinician from the very global to the really personal. It became my focus for students in their second to last quarter of internship. I tried to normalize that this is part of the work to constantly address. It seemed that the more normalized it became, the less students personalized the experience as some kind of moral failure.

The experience of traumatic stress for clinicians is influenced by many factors. Washington State, where I have practiced since 2001, has had some of the worst mental health funding in the country, even before the system all over the US went into collapse. This impacts student interns in that the schooling is designed for students to practice on what is known as "the worried well," yet students rarely have the opportunity to work with clients with the ego strength to be positively impacted by Jungian Dream work or attachment-based couples counseling, all the fun techniques you learn in graduate school and want to try. The reality is that the settings where students are placed in their internships have clients with multiple, chronic, and extreme mental health issues. The work, thus, is at best about basic stabilization, and students quickly become frustrated.

As an art therapist, I tried to help my students process their frustrations using visual prompts as much as possible.

An example would be to make two images/lists

1. What I get from being a therapist?
2. What is taken out of me from being a therapist?

The longer I taught, the more prompts and practices I came up with to explore the experience of Vicarious Trauma. When I transitioned from half-time teaching and half-time private practice to full-time private practice, I had time to develop a six-hour continuing education presentation on this subject that calls to me so loudly. This book is the transformation of that workshop to the page.

Here is a collection of how five theories in psychology address this issue, according to me. There are many models out there, and I offer you this buffet. It is my hope that one or two of the concepts or exercises will ring true for you and you can return to them again and again when you feel the work has become too much.

Each of the five sections has at least one exercise to try and a painting of mine that is my response to that prompt. For Psychoanalytic theory, the concept is to think about "Staying on the Boat." With Jungian theory, I ask you to see yourself as a rescuer and then separately as a professional. In Feminist theory, you are asked to be an activist outside of the office. In the section on Narrative theory, you see how I feel the work has impacted my ability to be alone. Finally, in considering Mindfulness work, I ask you to create a bubble of safety around you.

This is a marathon, not a sprint. I have found it pays off to take things slowly and let the concepts sink in. Also, you may be taking the Heroine's journey and come back to certain exercises or images again and again: when your personal life creeps into your professional life; when a client really gets under your skin; when a client suicides; when you get certified in a new style of therapy and feel like you're learning everything anew.

Although this book was written from my viewpoint as a therapist, the concepts apply to many fields. I hope teachers, first responders, clergy, activists, lawyers, anyone who cannot shake their work when they get home will find this book helpful. It can be read straight through, but you may experience it the way I enjoy Lynda Barry's *What It Is* and just open to any page and see what is there for you on that day.

Use individually, with clients, in groups, in supervision.

Enjoy!

This book offers a look at
Vicarious Trauma
through five theoretical lenses.
Psychoanalytic, Jungian, Feminist,
Narrative and Mindfulness.
This follows my own journey
as a therapist.

And now a classic parable, used to explore the experience of Vicarious Trauma. I even Illustrated it.

Jack wants more from life, and he cashes in his biggest resource for something that may or may not work out. Once those seeds get planted, they grow beyond what is known, and it becomes a crazy, often scary adventure, with lots of pitfalls and no clear escape route. But then, through all the chaos and yelling about being consumed, our hero begins to see things that will change their life for the better—a goose that only lays golden eggs when a golden harp is played. Jack just has to figure out how to outrun a giant, while carrying a goose and a harp, while climbing down an unruly giant vine. In most versions, Jack chops down the tree so that his demons do not follow him. In my version, the tree still stands, we just have enough distance from it as to not be overwhelmed by what lives in it.

That thing you planned,
in a hopeful state,
has grown beyond
what you can control,
and is taken you places
you did not want
to go.

Our Growth

We find our hero
wants more out of life.

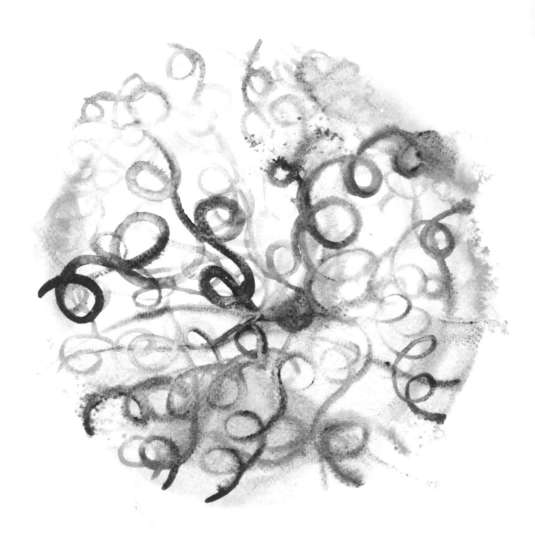

They buy the seeds to
their dream.

But it grows into something
they could not have imagined
.

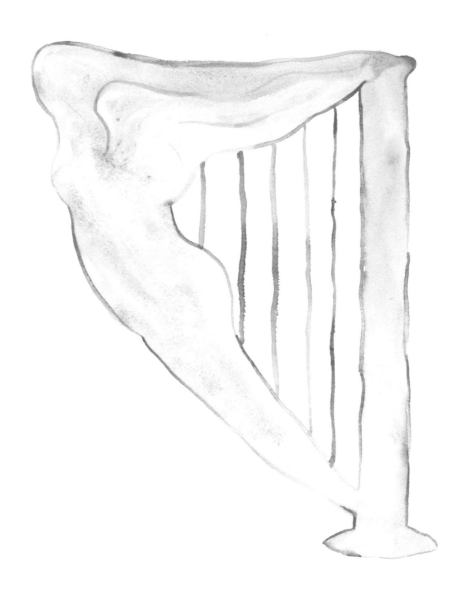

To get through it, they have to give
the journey all their time and energy

They find a way to own this
New identity.

It is Christmas Eve at the Day
Program for Chronically Mentally ill adults.
A client comes in and requests
a bag a food because the program
will be closed for several day.
It is here that she gets a
freshly cooked lunch four days a week.
Her case manager has told us
not to give her food to take home
because she trades it for beer.
He reports to us that all that is
in her tiny room is a bare mattress
and cans of beer.
None of the other staff is around.
I know I'll get in trouble later but
I give her a bag a food.
When I was young and we were
on food stamps, we learned the
hard way that not every Grocery
took them.
The teller shoos us away.
The full, packed bag sits on
the counter. But we have
No way to pay for it.

Know when
your own
Stuff
is being
Triggered

Bessel van der Kolk, M.D. has given us this model of what happens to the brain during a traumatic situation. It is why when you are in a high-pressure situation, you feel like you are working with your most basic skills.

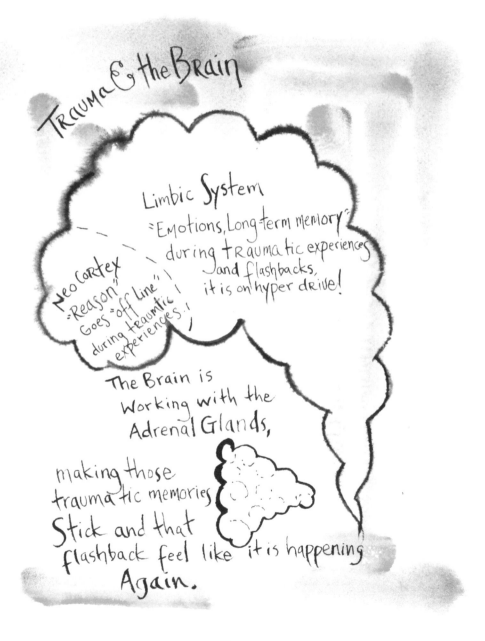

Psychoanalytic

Psychoanalytic theory would see vicarious trauma as countertransference, an experience of the clinician being impacted by the client as his/her/their own issues are being triggered. Transference is what the client imagines and projects on to the therapist. Countertransference occurs when the counselor loses their ability to keep a sense of distance in the work and becomes overwhelmed hearing a client's story or finds that they take the work home with them and can not shake off the stories. The therapists should cope with this by doing their own therapy.

When I was trained in this style, there was a fetishized therapist often discussed who was always appropriately distant from his work. What this ideal does not address is that the work is just plain stressful and anyone would crack in many of the situations clinicians face. There are some folks I have met along the way, who have enough money to pamper themselves and vacation frequently, whose own lives had so little trauma and few stressors that they are able to float through the work.

This book is not for that person. This book is for those of us that have led complex lives and now need to be able make a living over a lifetime doing good work in the world.

Psychoanalytic theory has some good stuff. When I was in graduate school, we would be lectured *ad nauseam* to be like a *tree* in the session. At the time, I had no idea what was being asked of me, but now I understand that we were being told to be grounded, to let the client have the depth of their own experience and know that they have the ability to change. Their process may be at a pace slower then you could have ever imagined, but this is their journey. It is your job as a clinician to hold a space, nonjudgmental and steady, informative and calm, that can allow change to take place. The "talking cure" is alive and well.

Since the tree metaphor fell flat with me, I tried a different one when I was teaching. I asked my students to "stay on the boat." The idea being that at their internships, they are finally in the role of therapist and incredibly excited to be helpful. Some clients would feel they had a special bond with the beginning therapist and would suggest that if that clinician just went a little further than their role allowed—spent a little extra time, shared a few personal stories, bought them a nice piece of clothing, introduced them to some stable people—the client would surely get and stay better on their watch (yes, all these things really happened).

When I heard these stories, I would erupt with my catchphrase, "Stay On The Boat! You can throw out a life ring, but if you get in the water what will happen?" Everyone would nod, and some would say back, "You'll get pulled under."

"Yes", I say, "down you go and now you can not help anyone." And what you need to be learning early in your career is not how to be seen as extremely special by one client, but how to be an average general therapist to lots of clients. Then, I would end this speech with one of my other key catchphrases, "I have spoken." This might have been why some students loved me and others tried to get me fired.

Exercises

Throughout the book you'll find exercises to complete
to guide you through your own healing process.

Can you heal the split?

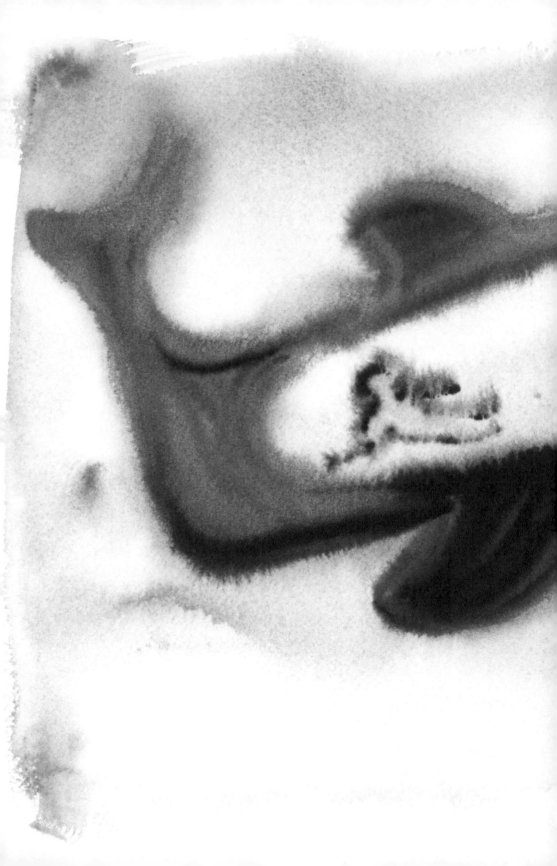

I found
Myself
in the
Belly of the
Whale.

Fresh out of graduate school
with a Masters degree in Art Therapy.
Tens of thousands of dollars in debt,
I was lucky to have a job but....
the head administrator hated Me...
most of the other clincians had been
there 20 years and were in their
own servival bubbles and the
clients had so Many extreme
problems. I felt hopeless.

They find a way to own this
New identity.

Stay ON the Boat

Can you stay grounded in your own experience while being with others?

Jungian

Carl Jung believed that within every client was a wounded healer and within every clinician was a wounded client. He believed it was these wounds that drew us to the profession and the understanding of these wounds that made us better clinicians.

> "I was working with homeless youth—many of whom had traumatic backgrounds, dual diagnoses, self-harming and were often suicidal. For several months I had low energy, wasn't able to sleep well the nights before I worked, I was avoiding seeing my friends and always had an upset stomach. I did enjoy the work. I think that's why it was so hard to see I was wearing myself out."

This letter was sent to me after I spoke on the podcast *Psychology in Seattle* on Vicarious Trauma. It is a perfect summary of what I know many clinicians experience. There is a lot of discussion about self care—take a bath, journal, remember to take a lunch—but there is not much looking at the deeper dynamics that make the work exhausting. The concept that we are not saviors but good enough witnesses can be difficult to swallow and do five days a week.

In Jungian theory, you find a way to reconciliation of opposites. For example, all of us have a shadow self that is working against us, and the way forward is to befriend that shadow. There is focus in Jungian therapy on tolerating personal suffering, finding the capacity to endure, and trusting we can live through these times, as generations before us have.

Finally, Jungian theory emphasizes the ability to live with things that seem not to fit together, that seem opposite and know that is tolerable, maybe not the most fun you have ever had but something you can live through.

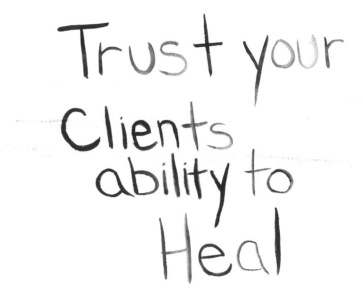

Exercises

- Create your wounded healer.
- Image the hero's journey you have been on.
- Create a list of the strength your clients have, that have gotten them this far.

The Jungian archetype for the
Wounded healer is
Chiron, the first centaur

They were a great teacher
and immortal.

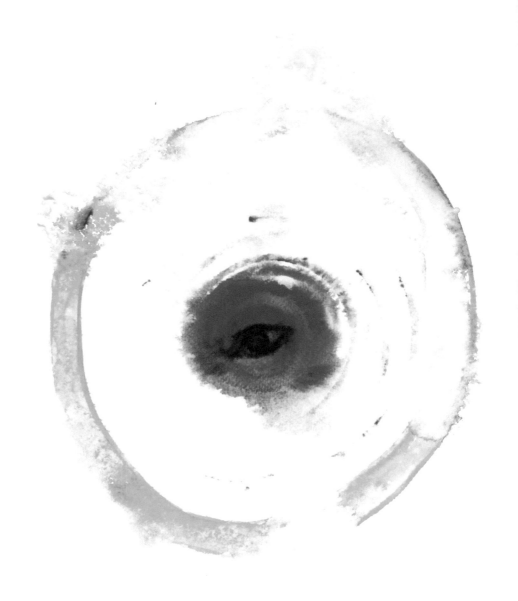

Once, they were injured in battle.

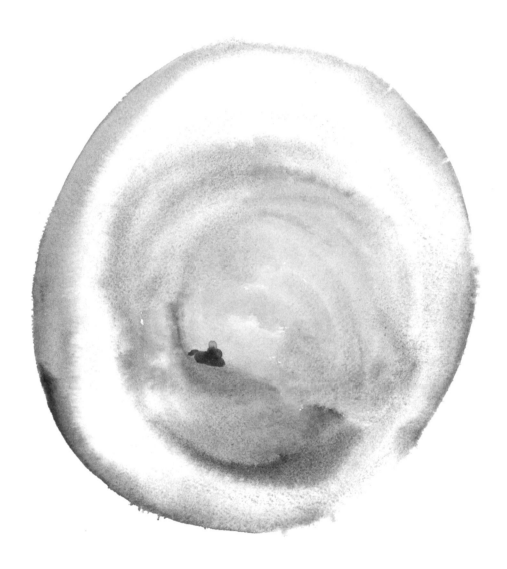

They went into a deep cave to heal.

It was there they realized they had
to become mortal
to truly heal.

The places where we get stuck, drained, lonely.

One way I frame it, is we are stuck in the tension between that part of us that wants to be seen as a professional and that part of our selves that just wants to rescue people and have the story move along at a fast pace and wrap up with a happy ending.

The tension between two identities the Professional/the Rescuer.
Make an image of yourself as a professional...

And the rescuer…

Feminist

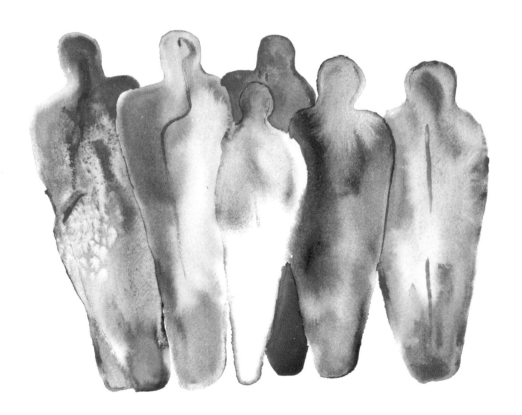

Breath in
with the Goddess
and out
with the patriarchy

Feminist theory changed the way psychology was viewed. If the personal is political as Gloria Steinem said, then there is a whole list of things you can talk about that had been previously viewed as unmentionable. If we are following Audre Lorde's lead and dismantling the master's house with tools not of his inventing, then the game is going to change. Things are going to get interesting, real, painful, and very very brave.

As Judith Herman was training to be a doctor, she noticed that many of her patients spoke about being sexually abused by their fathers, but when she went to the literature, she found nothing on the subject. There was no acknowledgement that many people have experienced sexual abuse and that it impacted every aspect of their lives. She went on to write several books on the topic of trauma. Her model first admits that trauma happens and lays out that it can become part of our story and we can still go on to live full and productive lives. Her book *Trauma and Recovery* has been translated into ten languages. The following images are concepts she introduced into the lexicon.

Hyperarousal....
The sense of being in
Extreme Danger...

Dr. Judith Herman pioneered the idea that abuse impacted people and they could recover from those experiences.

Re-Experiencing:
The moment of
Trauma
is right under
the surface
of your
skin.

3 Stage process of
Healing & Recovery

1. Establish Safety

2. Remembering & Morning

3. Reconnecting

— Judith Herman
    Trauma & Recovery 1992

Exercises

Create an image of your client healing from the outside in.

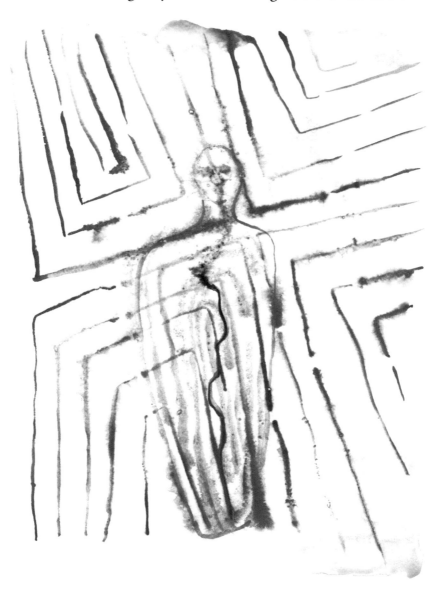

Trust that your client is learning & growing as fast as They Can

Dr. Herman's model also moves us out of the practice room. We have to take what we have known, seen, and heard and find our way to activism. That will look different ways for different people. Are you blogging about mental health issues? Are you writing your legislators? Are you speaking out in professional settings against racism?

Create an image of your inner and/or outer activist.

Use Your Voice for Social Change

"It is a competency-based paradigm that perceives human beings as responsive to the problems of their lives, capable of solving those problems, and desirous of change. It is also a politically informed model that always observes human experience within the framework of societal and cultural realities."

-Laura Brown, Ph.D

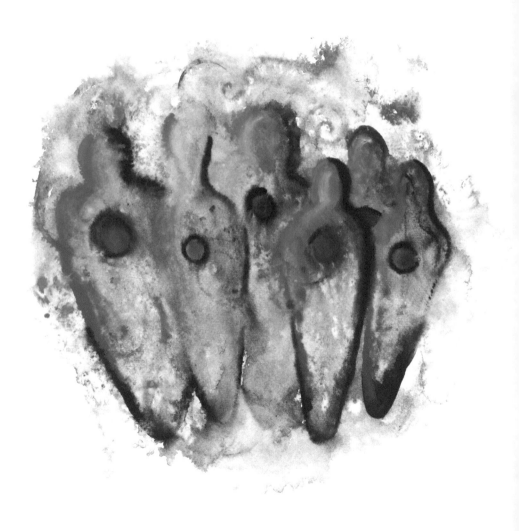

Create a sign and bring it to a protest:

Narrative

In an academic paper that looked at 38 published studies examining professionals indirectly exposed to trauma through their therapeutic work with trauma victims, the two factors that increased people's experiences of Vicarious Trauma the most were large caseloads with mostly traumatized clients and the clinician having personal trauma history. And, the two things that had the greatest impact on making people feel better were support from work colleagues and support at home.

Throughout researching for a six-hour presentation on Vicarious Trauma that I offered to clinicians in the Seattle area, I learned of countless tests and models for clinicians to address their experience. But when I asked around, none of the therapists I met had ever heard of them.

Karen W. Saakvinte's work was the most impactful to me. The nine questions that she developed take the experience of Vicarious Trauma from the global to the very personal. In answering them, people tend to find the one or two places where they are the most wounded and can really focus in on healing those rifts.

Exercises

Thank to Karen Saakvitne, Ph.D,
we have these NINE questions:

How does your work impact how
   you see the world?

Your spiritual beliefs?

Your sense of self, groundedness
      & emotional stability?

Your sense of personal safety
      & your families safety?

The way you judge people?

Your sense of control?

Your ability to be alone or with others?

Your relationship to your body?
               (an illistration in two parts)

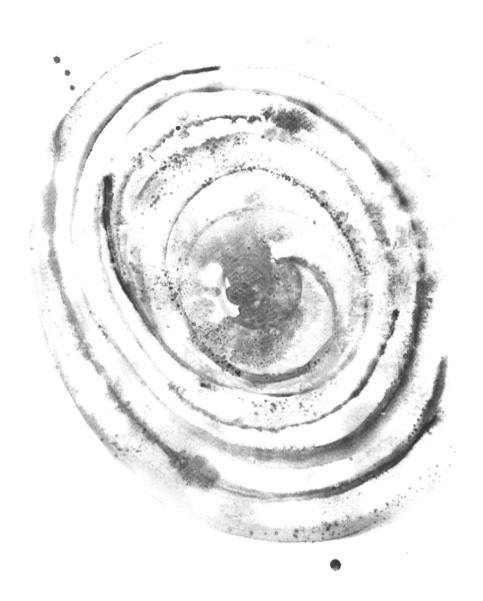

World

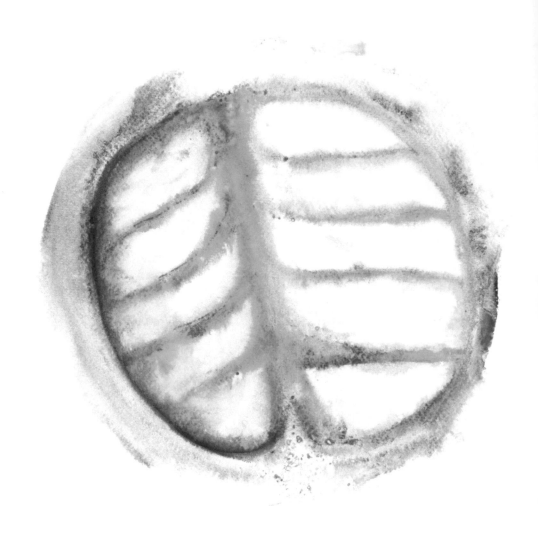

Spiritual

Grounded

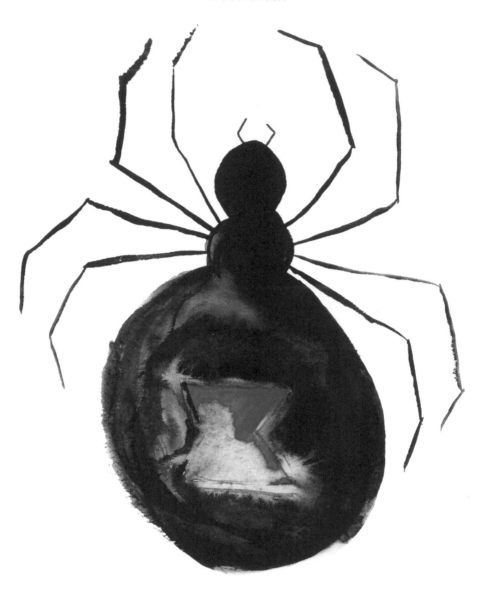

Sense of safety

Judge people

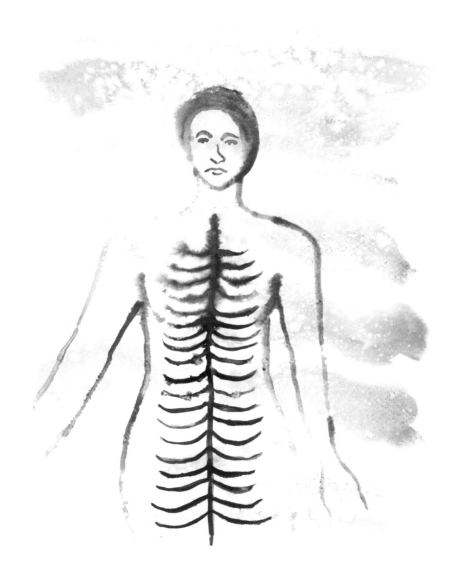

Control

Ability to be alone

Body in 2 parts

Body

Mindfulness

When we feel overwhelmed, we often do whatever we can to avoid difficult feelings. We do not want to suffer. But sometimes, in avoidance of suffering, we numb ourselves and thereby create new problems. My experience of Mindfulness-based work was brought into focus when I studied Pat Ogden's Sensorimotor Psychotherapy model. Much of the trainings were about slowing down and moving away from the story we always tell and into exploring five-sense perception—moving away from telling the trauma story in the same way and instead being aware of sight, sounds, temperature, and taste, in the moment. When you think of a client that's hard for you to work with, does your posture change, does your body temperature change, do you have a flash of memory, or a literal bad taste in your mouth? In mindfulness, you stay with these experiences and just notice. By finding space in the moment, by increasing our mindful perception, we reduce our suffering because we find a way to tolerate what once seemed intolerable.

The Tower, things feel like they are falling apart

Trauma

Fight Fiight

FREEZE

CRY

—Pat Ogden, Ph.D.

By naming the common experience connected with trauma, we decrease shame and find that healing is possible. When you experience trauma, it is perfectly normal to experience or act on the desire to fight, to run, to freeze or to cry. No one way is more valid than another. We are wired to do all of them. Our culture may put greater value on one over another, but that does a great disservice to us all. If you have been frozen after a client disclosed trauma, know it is a totally normal response. If you have cried all the way home from work, know we have all been there.

By slowing down, you can gain a sense of clarity about your experience.

In mindfulness-based therapy, experiences are slowed down with the help of our senses. We observe, in the moment. The "story" of what happened becomes secondary to how you feel right now. Does just thinking of the trauma make you feel hot or see red? In this work, you stay with those early signals for as long as there is important information there. We get out of our heads and into our bodies, allowing different aspects of the story to come forward.

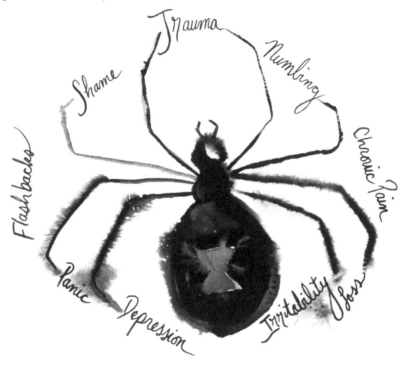

—Dr. Janina Fisher

By normalizing the experience of trauma, and decreasing shame, we are able to integrate Traumatic experiences.

Trauma survivors often experience a cluster of responses, and everyone has their own set. You may find yourself having flashbacks to that bad job with the unsupportive boss and lean heavily on drinking to numb yourself whereas your coworker may always be panicked and in this weird shame dynamic that makes no sense to you. Same monster, many heads. You are both caught in the same web, just entangled in different strands. Dr. Janina Fisher's work offers wonderful models of these different manifestations of trauma and how we get stuck in a web of shame.

The experience of attunement happens when you connect authentically, in a calm way, with another person. When practicing mindfulness and learning to be centered, it is helpful to practice in a space and with people who offer you a feeling of groundedness. This is someone you breathe easy around, this is a space in which you can comfortably close your eyes, a place where you can be still.

Exercises

Practicing mindfulness when looking at vicarious trauma:

- Create a protective bubble around yourself.
- How big it is?
- Does it start close to your body or do you need it to start far away?
- What color is it inside, and what color is it outside?
- What is the temperature and texture like inside?
- To make it protective, how hard or soft would it need to be?

Make a bubble of protection.
How big is it?
What color is it, inside and out?
What temperature is it?
How does it taste and smell?

Tell yourself you're doing a good job, then feel your reaction.

- Do you agree or disagree with this statement?
- Why or why not?

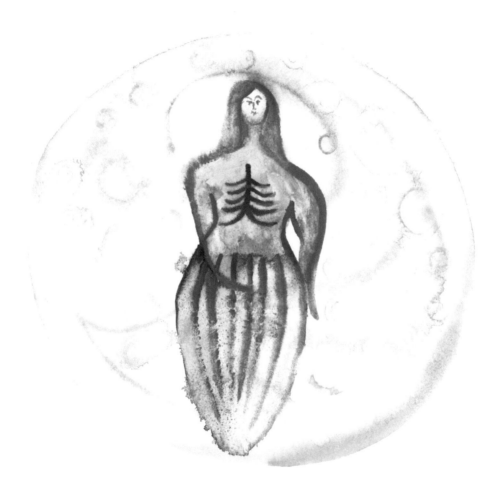

Take a breath, smile and say, "I am doing a good job."
How does thay feel? How do you Know?

Conclusion

Ok, we just went on a ride. How are you doing? I hope you show someone you trust some of your responses. Next steps may be finding a group of like-minded folks to keep having these conversations. Maybe you get into a peer supervision group or, like me, paint as much as you can. You may be ready to make your own graphic novel about your experience; please do, the world needs it.

Keep making art.

All my love,
Rebecca

Finding Self Regulation with others seeking Self Regulation

References

Hensel, JM1, Ruiz C, Finney C, Dewa CS. "Meta-analysis of risk factors for secondary traumatic stress in therapeutic work with trauma victims." J Trauma Stress. 2015 Apr; 28(2):83-91.

Millard, Emma Louise. (2017) *A mixed methods approach investigating cognitive changes in vicarious trauma within trainees and qualified therapists.* DClinPsy thesis, University of Nottingham.

Herman, Judith. *Trauma and Recovery.* Basic Books, 1992.

Mauger, Benig. "Chiron in the 21st century: Wounded Healers Today." *Inside Out* Issue 71: Autumn 2013.

Saakvinte, Karen W. and Laurie Anne Pearlman. *Transforming the Pain: A Workbook on Vicarious Traumatization.* Norton Professional Books,1996.

Ogden, Pat, Kekuni Minton, and Claire Pain. *Trauma and the Body: A Sensorimotor Approach to Psychotherapy. W. W. Norton and Co., 2006.*

van der Kolk, Bessel. *The Body Keeps the Score. Viking, 2014.*

The images in this book are are watercolors painted by me, using the techniques featured in *Watercolor Made Simple* by Claudia Nice

Rebecca Bloom is a board certified art therapist and licensed mental health counselor with a private practice in Seattle, WA. She paints, presents on trauma and rescues terriers.

www.bloomcounseling.com

on Instagram @rtext

on Twitter @rbloomatr

on facebook @squarethecircleworkbook

CPSIA information can be obtained
at www.ICGtesting.com
Printed in the USA
BVHW060345200619
551414BV00005BA/50/P

* 9 7 8 1 6 4 4 3 8 6 3 9 2 *